Tasting Precious Metal

ALSO BY DANNY DOVER

Kindness Soup, Thankful Tea (chapbook, 2006)

TASTING PRECIOUS METAL

Poems by

Danny Dover

Danny Dover

Antrim House

Simsbury, Connecticut

Library of Congress Control Number: 2014937557

ISBN: 978-1-936482-67-2

Printed & bound by United Graphics, Inc.

Book design by Rennie McQuilkin

Photographs for cover and text by Bob Eddy & Tim Calabro
Randolph, VT (www.FirstLightStudios.net)

Author photograph by Mary Swartz

Antrim House
860.217.0023
AntrimHouse@comcast.net
www.AntrimHouseBooks.com
21 Goodrich Road, Simsbury, CT 06070

ACKNOWLEDGMENTS

Grateful aknowledgment to editors of the following publications, in which some of the poems in this book first appeared, often in earlier versions:

Birchsong: "A Bat Is living," "Gathering," "Tractor Man"

Bloodroot Literary Magazine: "Above the Dental Office," "Color Wars," "Letter to My Nose," "My People," "NYC, 1956," "Quaker Oats Box," "A State of Kansas," "Time Machine," "Virgin Mary," "Yukon Territory"

Several of the poems in this volume appeared in *Kindness Soup, Thankful Tea: Selected Poems by Danny Dover* (Dhotarap Press, 2006): "Cake," "Cigarette," "Honestly Now," "Hummingbird," "Old Friends," "Pandemic," "Perfect Storm," "Recipe for Relaxing with Men," "Rose," "Stone Wall," and "Teddi's Garden."

*   *   *

Special thanks to: Eric Webb, Don Collins, Sandy Lincoln, Danny Murphy, Dick & Dorothy Robson, Mindy Branstetter, George Lister, Rolf Olsen, and Jay Cary for your honest feedback and suggestions over the years. Thanks also to the Vermont Men's Tribe, the Lampshade Poets, Marjorie Ryerson, M. D. Drysdale, Tom Slayton, and dozens of readers and friends too numerous to mention here.

To my wife, Mary Swartz, for your sharp mind and keen ear. You are my dearly trusted filter and gatekeeper for emerging poems.

In memory of 'Do' Roberts, founder and publisher of *Bloodroot,* who passed away as this book was going to print. Her generosity of spirit and passion for creative writing were a huge inspiration to us all.

My deep gratitude to Bob Eddy and Tim Calabro at First Light Studios for the excellent cover and text photos.

To Rennie McQuilkin of Antrim House: your unremitting attention to detail and commitment to quality have made me a much better writer.

TABLE OF CONTENTS

I. TIME MACHINE

Prologue: Freight / 2
My People / 3
Voice Letter, 1943 / 4
Perfect Storm / 6
Quaker Oats Box / 7
Cigarette / 9
NYC, 1956 / 11
Cookie / 12
A State of Kansas / 14
Time Machine / 16
Color Wars / 18
A Letter to My Nose / 19

II. ANOTHER COUNTRY

Stone Wall / 22
Thank You, Kyama / 23
When Nature Calls / 25
Another Country / 26
Dipika's Walk / 27
Ms. Liberty / 28
Republican Primary Season, 2012 / 30
Doing the Crosswords with Bill Clinton / 32
Pandemic / 33
Huevos Revueltos / 35

III. CALCULUS OF LOSS

Flood / 38
Breakfast with Buzz / 40
After the Flood / 41
Famine Grounds / 43
Rose / 44
Teddi's Garden / 46
Calculus of Loss / 47
Moonlight / 49
Nothing Is Lost / 51

IV. ALMOST FORGIVEN

Oh Canada / 54
Above the Dental Office / 56
Winter Affair / 58
Amanita / 59
Shopping Days / 60
Therapy / 61
Jesus of Comcast / 62
Love / 63
Budget / 64
Virgin Mary / 66

V. TASTING PRECIOUS METAL

Gathering / 70
Cake / 71
Grazing / 73
A Bat Is Living / 74
Snake Skin / 75
Laptop / 76
Handball / 77
Recipe for Relaxing with Men / 78
Old Friends / 80
Tractor Man / 82
Dancing Girls / 83
Playground / 84
Chickadees / 85
Honestly Now / 86
Hummingbird / 87
Keno Hill, 1972 / 89
Yukon Territory / 90

NOTES / 92

ABOUT THE AUTHOR / 95

ABOUT THE BOOK / 96

A man doesn't have time in his life
to have time for everything.
He doesn't have seasons enough to have
a season for every purpose . . .
A man needs to love and to hate at the same moment,
to arrange and confuse, to eat and to digest
what history takes years and years to do. . .

from "A Man in His Life," Yehuda Amichai

I. TIME MACHINE

Freight

Heavy freight cars
glide by our café window
festooned in costumes
of bold graffiti
Please pass something lighter
you plead as my burdensome
prose derails at your feet

Words often roll out of me that way
all fat-cartoon-font-and-primary-color
blustering down a wide track
on well-greased wheels

Yet now and then I awake
in puzzled awe of the vagrant
who's been prowling through
my dreams again
leaving provocative scrawl
sprayed over my rusty imagination

My People

My New York clan
were short solid stock
cut close to the ground
by the wars of Europe,
their bubbly voices
fizzing like seltzer
in over-heated apartments,
ambitions stored away
with musty dress suits –
Uncle Phil strumming in
a mandolin orchestra,
Uncle Meyer's
meager grocery and
Yiddish poems, tiny
chain-smoking Aunt
Fika primping wavy
salt-and-pepper hair
and Uncle Sol,
Uncle Sol who fled
Germany before the war –
these were my People,
my ports-of-call riding
the wild seas of the '60s
who taught of times
you must make yourself
invisible to survive,
Uncle Sol, through misty
spectacles staring past my chin
into the face of 1937 Berlin –
The Nazis are coming,
you'll see, Sol chanted,
you'll see, you'll see.

Voice Letter, 1943

You slot a dime
in a novelty machine
at the officers' club
of a Southern boot-camp,
recording the lines
of a lonely soldier
far from home
and off to war,
a shy and tongue-tied
Brooklyn Jew
prattling on
to a faithful wife
and baby girl
about shrimp creole
and wax museums
with an awkward
cadence and tenderness
enshrined in grooves
on a vinyl disc.
And from this
single fragment

of the sound of you
I would gather
every syllable,
each stammered phrase
and nervous laugh,
like chromosomes
from a strand of hair
to resurrect you

standing now
in front of me —
not yet my father,
young enough
to be my son —
a handsome boy
full of pride
and youthful bluster
running out of time,
forever searching
for what could
be spoken.

Perfect Storm

Sunday night in the 50s
in the attic TV room,
my family, stowaways
in our tiny cabin
bathed in gray cathode beams
announcing impending hurricanes:
Steve Allen. Jackie Gleason.
Sid Caesar. George Burns.
Headed our way, duly warned.
Prepare.

Secured by Mother's heaving breast,
steady engine rhythms signal
safe at sea, sails down, winds calm,
we have weathered worse together.

When it comes, a distant roar, surfing,
swirling, moaning, cracking, wide
waves of wild mirth wash over,
gasping for air, foaming, open-mouthed,
my father, ruby-faced, tear-choked, a thin
high cackle, mother's chest

rumbling, rolling, lifeboat
tossing, groaning, hanging on
for dear life, riding out
the blessed storm,
my little body drenched

in the sweet and salient,
holy laughter of my family.

Quaker Oats Box

As a boy I recall
listless mornings
staring over
steaming bowls
of pasty cereal
at a stern-faced Quaker
gazing back
from a rigid frame

until the day I thought
the Quaker blinked
And in that moment

eyeing the Quaker
with a box in his hand
with a picture of a Quaker
with a box in his hand
with a picture of a Quaker
with a box in his hand

I soared on a journey
through portals and portals
within portals in portals
past endless strings
of luminous pearls
stretched out
in vast and infinite space
skipping like a stone
toward the rarest glimpse
of something sublime
and forever unknowable

then returned to breakfast

to resume my day
alone and dazed
too young for the language
of life-changing wonder

Cigarette

Smoking cigarettes
when I was eight
but never inhaling,
we were fire-carriers,
smoke-blowers, down sidewalks
and in bathrooms and woods,
snitching from your purse,
a dirty secret 'til
your highbeams in my deer face
one evening at dinner:

I hear you've been smoking.
Go light one up
and let's talk.

In the kitchen chair
and fluorescent glare
my tremorous smirk,
your steady stare,
uncharted terrain for
mother and son:

Now don't you look ridiculous.

Which is when the phone rang
and you left me
and the floor left
with you, Mother — you took
the chairs and lights
the walls and table and
all the air and most of

my meager body with you
into the other room, leaving
only this floating
hand, not mine, holding
a stick of fire
in an airless black cave
where I had vaporized,
a single strand of smoke
still rising from the very
last cigarette of my life.

So, Mother, here's to you and
the awesome power of your shaming,
a dangerous weapon, but laser-focused
and wielded with love and wisdom,
a surgical tweak to a tender mind,
my only wish now, to bring you back

to our kitchen where I'll gather
all the abusers and bombers,
makers of missiles and landmines,
mutilators and leaders,
the ones with triggers
and smoke and fire
upon their fingers,
just once to face
your Spartan stare:

Now don't you look ridiculous.

NYC, 1956

I'm a child staring at a news map
of Midtown as atomic target
imagining circles of fire
rippling out from a dark stone
dropped into Manhattan's
gaping mouth, mouthing
megaton as a silent mantra,
considering the new word
the way a tongue
considers a chipped
tooth, the way Herbert's
face was considering
death when I saw him,
when his heart
burst like a bomb.

Cookie

She was my first pet I named for my sister's boyfriend and future ex-husband
who took me to ballgames & Coney Island the way I knew my father should
from seeing *Father Knows Best* his nickname was Cookie from that year's
hit tune *Cookie Cookie Lend Me Your Comb* Cookie was blue and white
and gurgled gorgeous songs from an endless parakeet repertoire
I learned what I could and sang along with Cookie
perched on my finger so close to my mouth
it felt sexy in a sort of eight-year-old's
idea of sexy Cookie
was free to
fly when I
came home from
school she could see from
the window and fly downstairs
to greet me at the door full of song
and fresh poop perched on my head I dreamed
over and over of a skiing parakeet by my side my best
friend my pet my buddy complete with thimble-sized wool
cap singing down the mountain together hundreds of times I ran
Cookie through a maze of mirrors made for Mr. Fernhoff's science class
project to see if she was smarter than a hamster named Schlep before Tony
stepped on Schlep one rainy Sunday I used Cookie for target practice
with a rubber dart gun she was on top of the cage across the room
and BLAM I got her good she fell behind the dresser stunned
but came back from the dead lying there in my shaking
hands and eventually forgave me Cookie was
my first lover I found the little nest
of chewed up book covers
behind World Book
Encyclopedias

A through
G where she
had laid one perfect
egg I was completely baffled
there was no other parakeet in the
house so I must be the father I thought
from Cookie tenderly pecking the salty skin
of my nose all those times we crooned and gurgled
together face to face in our most intimate moments that
is how the DNA transferred even though I never heard of DNA
I knew there had to be a boy & a girl and I didn't know how to tell
my parents holding the pale blue egg and wondering at the miracle that
broke in my clumsy fingers warm yolk running down my wrist and
oh how I sobbed for the loss of my unborn parakeet child

A State of Kansas

When entering into
the state of Kansas
you might go as a boy
in the summer of '58
from the Land of Oz
in a darkened theater
to a bright back seat
of the family Ford
rolling west toward
the promise of grand
canyons and disneylands
but first must cross
the state of Kansas.
So you take your post
as sleepless sentinel
while parents fuss
with speed limits and maps,
nose pressed to glass
scouring vast prairie skies
for an innocent puff
of smoky cloud
that could be the child
of a hideous vortex
hunting you down
over four hundred miles
to the Colorado line —
a lifetime for a boy
in the summer of '58.
Then decades swirl by
yet still you dodge
the twisting demons

beyond your view,
driving and driving
the length and girth
of well-worn roads,
perpetual traveler in
a state of kansas.

Time Machine

Only eleven and I am truly lost
eyes spinning like caged hamsters
spongy hands and flushed face
My first date

impossibly tall
Laura Jean blue-eyed
goddess of auburn hair hung
in perfect hip-long braids
from a high-born tower
begging to be climbed
until one sweaty afternoon in 1959

hauling myself up hand-over-hand
toward her broad freckled forehead
to share a large orange soda
in a phantom theater far below
the matinee of *Time Machine*
unwinding itself
in the cool artificial night

as we blast off through bits
of popcorn and Mars bars
beyond silky braids
and super-charged
naked elbows
landing gently
on warm moist ground
a future landscape
not yet known

Sue Ellen Thompson

Co Co Beaux

Danny Dover

November 7, 2014

The Arts Café

Now in its 21th year, the mission of The Arts Café Mystic is to contribute to the cultural life of Southeastern Connecticut by presenting programs featuring readings by the nation's most celebrated poets and writers, complemented by music from New England's finest musicians. The Arts Café is a recipient of the Dorothy Mullen Arts and Humanities Award to "honor the most innovative and effective arts and humanities programs across the nation."

Board of Directors

John Sutherland, President
William Grady
Wendy Halsey
Patricia Kitchings (Honorary)
Susan Moffett
Dorothea Moore
Ben Philbrick
Elizabeth Raisbeck
Paulann Sheets
Christie Max Williams

Volunteers

Winslow Anderson	Claire Cooney
Sita Cooney	Christopher Greenleaf
Wendy Halsey	Sibby Lynch
Jim Marshall	Bill Moffett
Cate Moffett	Susan Moffett
Dorothea Moore	Elizabeth Raisbeck

Program designed by CMB Creative Group

In Gratitude

The Arts Café wishes to thank the following friends for their generous support. Their generosity directly translates into programs presenting the nation's most celebrated poets and New England's finest musicians.

Poets Laureate Circle ($1000-$5,000)
Alan Belzer & Susan Parker Martin
Bill & Christine Grady
Chester W. Kitchings Foundation
Wally Lamb
John & Sue Sutherland
Whaler's Inn

Troubador's Circle ($500 to $999)
Nan & Ted Danforth
Dorothea Moore
John Racanelli & Betty Medsger
Elizabeth Raisbeck & Zell Steever
Paulann Sheets
Sandy & Sidney Van Zandt
Christie Max Williams & Catharine Moffett

Bard's Circle ($250 to $499)
Dr. Ranjna Bindra
Lynn & Jeff Callahan
Marjorie Farmer & Valerie Popkin
Kathleen Kucka & John Sutter
Susan Moffett
Thomas & Marguertie Moore
Jane Percy
Annie & Ben Philbrick

Sonneteers Circle ($100 to $249)

Antonio Design Group
Tom & Kathrine Bishop
Dan & Jane Brannegan
Cask 'n Keg
Elizabeth & Warren Clark
Courtyard Gallery
Timothy R. Cummings
Joseph & Jean Drake
Charlie & Michele Ewers
Margaret Gibson & David McKain
Diane Goldsmith & Linda Dolan
Jackie Gorman
Wendy Halsey
Owen & Nancy Hughes
Alex & Jan Hybel
Archie & Diane Leslie
Sarah Stifler Lucas
Melanie Greenhouse
David Madacsi
Jim Marshall
John & Marcia McGowan
Marilyn Nelson
Patty Oat
John & Julia Parry
Edwina Trentham & Greg Coleman
Frederick Turnbull
Kathy Weinberger & James Friedlander
Leslie Westhaver
Diana Hartwick Young
Susan Zimmerman & Claude Pellegrino

Rhymer's Circle (Less than $100)

Louise Andre
Anonymous

Natalie & Bill Billing
Bank Square Books
Natalie & Bill Billing
Tom & Melinda Blum
Roger Brown
Gill Castagna
Charlie Chase
Richard & Beth Close
Stuart Cole
Tom Couser & Barbara Zabel
Chris & Marie Cox
Dan Curland
Jeri DeSantis
Patricia & Robert Deskus
Gary & Janice Donovan
Arthur & Pamela Fox
Diane Goldsmith & Linda Doran
Marianne Grube
Frances Harkins
Barbara Heuer
Mike & Linda Hewitt
Sarah Janssens
Pamela Kent
Jonathan & Carol King
Mary Knight
Dan Leonard
Eugene & Carolyn LeRoy
Suzanne Levine & Lary Bloom
Eliza Linkemann
Maureen Logan
Louise Lumen
Robert & Tina MacBain
Mari Svensen MacPeek
Hiroko Masamune
Anne Matthews

Janet & Kennneth Mayer
Gae Melford
Peter & Ceseli Milstein
Janis Mink
Sabine Moffett
Thomsas & Marguerite Moore
Biddle & JoAnn Morris
Patty Oat
Lana Orphanides
Alicia Pena
Louise Ravsen
Jude Rittenhouse & Kurt Rauchenberger
Kenton Wing Robinson
Louise Roosen
Kimberly Ross
Leslie Sandin & Wayne Dailey
John & Janet McCaffrey Schloss
Paul & Sheila Scott
Julie Selwyn
Harold & Dora Slater
Jean-Yves & Elaine Solinga
Cheryl Sorensen
Patricia Sparkman
Paula & Bruce Stauffer
James Taylor & Clare Sheridan
Dr. George & Bianca Terranova
Edwina Trentham & Greg Coleman
Marya Ursin & Daniel Potter
Julia Van Dyke
Lissa Van Dyke
Roberta Vincent
Dave & Barbara Williams
Amy Young (In honor of Diana Hartwick Young)
Susan Zimmerman & Claude Pellegrino

M.C. Christie Max Williams

Opening Voice

Danny Dover is a Vermont-based poet who recently published his debut book *Tasting Precious Metal*, which has won accolades as "an expansive journey across the ranges of emotional terrain spanning loss, love, nostalgia, and wonder." Mr. Dover has worked as surveyor, foundry pattern-maker, folk singer, and dulcimer-maker, and was for many years the piano technician at Dartmouth College.

Music

Co Co Beaux is the beloved male a cappella group from Connecticut College. The award-winning ensemble has just released its eighth album *Key Change*, which includes songs by Bastille, Mumford & Sons, Rhianna, and Darius Rucker, among others.

Featured Poet

Sue Ellen Thompson has just published a new book of poems called *They*, which Wally Lamb has described as a "graceful and unforgettable collection." Ms. Thompson's previous book, *The Golden Hour*, was nominated for the Pulitzer Prize, as was her third volume, *The Leaving: New and Selected Poems*. Her first book, *This Body of Silk*, won the Samuel French Morse Prize. She has also won the Pablo Neruda Prize and the Maryland Author Award. Among her many other honors, she has been a Robert Frost Fellow at the Bread Loaf Writers' Conference and resident poet at the Frost Place in Franconia, New Hampshire. She also served as editor of the *Autumn House Anthology of Contemporary American Poetry*, which is taught in classrooms across the nation. Several of her poems have been read by Garrison Keillor on NPR's *The Writer's Almanac*.

Home

The place your parents brought you straight
from the hospital, where you spent
those endless years of grade-
school. Or maybe it's the place
where you raised your own
children, where you were never alone.
The place you retreat to after the divorce,
or when circumstances force
you to go there. According to Frost,
they have to – but you know the rest.

Who can say for how many weeks
after moving you will lie awake,
staring at the clock-radio, before
you stop listening for the pre-dawn roar
of traffic down your former street –
before the word begins to rise from deep
inside somewhere as you approach
the yellow blinker at Main and Oak,
which, like the porch light your mother
flicked off and on when you and your first lover
were parked at the darkest edge of the lawn,

reminds you where you belong.

Sue Ellen Thompson from *They*

not yet knowing
where to look
or who to ask
for directions
to our new
and permanent
addresses

Color Wars

I am a veteran of the Color Wars of
Lakeville Connecticut YMCA Camp
in the year mile-high bombs bloom
in Nevada deserts and we practice
diving under school desks when sirens
wail, way before 'Nam
the Blues against the Golds fighting for
points in foot races and rope-pulls
penalties for foul language and sloppy
beds bunkmate against bunkmate
I'm hiding behind enemy lines
the only Jew of three hundred boys
feeling neither golden nor blue but
maybe white eager to surrender
more taken with lanyards and toy
boats of pine scraps and pipe
cleaners than waging war a time
of life when the greatest ambition
is blending in to be just average
and not draw attention not like
my perfect two-point lay-up
once in gym class for the
wrong team

A Letter to my Nose

Let's be honest
it's been a difficult relationship
siblings joined at the face since birth
and you always charging into a roomful
of strangers one step ahead of me
introducing yourself to all the guests
before I've said a word
embarrassing really how brazen
you are standing naked
and unabashed
just breathing silently
and all eyes upon you
I shrink in your presence
although it hasn't always
been that way old photos
reveal a normal childhood
when you had
an appropriate place
grazing in a field of freckles
on my handsome face
but as we aged
some deep dysfunction
drove you to assert yourself
was it something I said
frostbite   too much pot smoke
I'll never know why
things got really ugly
as you enlarged
without my knowledge
at the same time
the rest of me was

diminishing a betrayal
unforgivable to this day
but family is family
and I can't deny that we
have to live together
so if it's not too late
let's call a truce
and begin a reconciliation
I want to believe we can
be beautiful again I'll start
with this poem as a tribute
to all the breathing you've
done for me without fail
even in dreams
with my faceless body
floating over foreign landscapes
on galactic voyages
that could've taken my breath away

II. ANOTHER COUNTRY

Stone Wall

for Urche's mother

You were not pretty, Urche's mother:
rugged, dark and dusty face
in a pale and yellow stubbled field,
scything barley since dawn.

Eye-to-eye across the wall,
with your steady gaze and
Dolpo tongue, the telling of it.

Yes, understood,
your awesome gift,
my precious son.
And the proud pain of it,
the loss of him beyond this wall,
thrust a thousand years
into your world, this

eager boy, astride the stones,
legs a-dangle, grinning, happy,
growing, generous,
galloping heart, little
rodeo rider,
no walls in sight.

Dhotarap, Dolpa, Nepal

Thank You, Kyama

for the tea
we actually hate
yak butter tea
and don't speak a word
of your language
our backs creak
stomachs turn
the room is cramped
water suspect
toilet strange
but you pour
we fake a smile
and sip some more
thank you Kyama

for the tea
your lack of guile
monstrous silver
turquoise jewelry
musky scent of yak wool
freshly spun as you squat
by the awful tea
thank you Kyama

for wind-worn
leathered chestnut cheeks
murmured mantras
full cup raised
thank you Kyama

for your son

thank you

for pouring him
in our lives
thank you Kyama

for the tea

Boudha, Nepal

When Nature Calls

There comes a time
when nature calls
from the thin warm skin
of a camping tent
and cracks you open,
squatting like an animal
under moon shadow,
under clear cold kingdoms
of countless stars,
under the rim of jagged peaks
in a village named *Center*
where you've circled back
to a boy at the center
of your heart,
to fields of rusty grass
and glacial riverbeds,
to the drum and rumble
of chanting monks
at midnight,
to dust and dung
and footprints pressed
into shifting sandstone
canyon trails.

Dhotarap valley, Nepal

Another Country

When living
in another country listen
for the murmur of child monks
running late for lessons
with their song
of slapping sandals
by an early morning window

Follow the weathered gaze
of an old woman walking
deep in prayer around
a white-washed temple
Wander in the dawn-lit
trails of her canyon'd face

Spread this mountain village
through your fingers
braiding its lustrous strands
into a thick cloak
of cedar smoke   wet slate
and mustard oil

Soak in every moment
Let your skin of paper
dissolve
in a steady warm
drizzle of attention
to the ten thousand
sensations

Dipika's Walk

for Dipika B.K. and the People's Revolution, Nepal, April 2006

Eight years since this moth
flew too close to a cooking fire
melting her baby feet into candle stubs,
a finer flame burns in her hot fierce face
each new morning as Dipika walks,
scraped and bruised, stiff and clumsy,
with a perilous gait across a gravel yard.

But also watch the warm
beam of her hazel eyes
dance a gleaming leaping stride,
bouncing beyond rooftops
this morning,
as Dipika walks.

And if this were night,
Dipika would glow her bright-blinking
breakfast-anytime neon smile.

Step inside now under that smile,
as if settling in a warm booth
with fresh coffee
and home-made pie.

You might never see her again,
might never again visit this city,
might even miss
down-street an entire nation
stumbling out of fire onto its feet
this morning,
as Dipika walks.

Ms. Liberty

I'm at the corner
of 1st and 70th
near a tall blonde
New York debutante
posturing her lithe body
like a princess in her realm
angled into the late-night breeze
in Gucci heels and gauzy gown
raising a slim white arm
like a torch to command
attention
from a row of taxis
revving engines
at the next traffic light

I've just left a party
for newly-wed children
of those same cab drivers
come back on night-shift
still high on whiskey
cousins   brothers   uncles
store-clerks   nannies   cooks
& cleaners   packs of children
running wild through purple
ballrooms pungent with curry
shy teens jangling bracelets
by a torch-lit dance floor
flirting in cheap black suits
and bright silk chubas
through a flashy night
of Hindi glitter and shots

of Johnnie Walker

to this street corner
as Ms. Liberty leans out
like the carved prow
of a trim ship ready
for the high tide of taxis
from a hundred nations
that will sweep down
the length of Manhattan
and float her safely out
to a harbor home
they've come to claim
as their own

and then beyond
back to beloved villages
where she'll be honored
at each house squatting
on earthen floors beside
dried-dung cooking fires
crowded by wide-eyed
children daring to touch
her smooth ghostly skin
glowing white as a torch
upon dim walls
of dry stone

Republican Primary Season, 2012

Not long ago in dead
of winter a lost flamingo
turned north and tumbled
from the sky over Siberia,
a shivering pink body
on spindly legs found
by startled villagers,
an exotic spectacle
they bundled in furs,
nursed with nettles
and warm yak milk
through sub-zero nights
by a spruce-fired stove,
and restored to health
for the hard journey home.

Our own flamingo beams
from a bare-limbed maple
in bright plastic exile
below the meadow
where it snagged
in flood waters
early last fall,
a welcome break

from the dull winter palette
of unease and isolation
that has settled upon us
once again,
when darkness portends
whatever shifting course

is feared the most
as if an entire nation —
tired and lost —
just dropped from the sky
without compass or map,
a colorful alien creature
waiting to be thawed out
with a little kindness
and sense of direction.

Doing the Crosswords
with Bill Clinton

How quickly the world shrinks
upon learning of his obsession
until here we are, hunkered down
on my couch, each with a Sunday
New York Times in tandem focus
while Bill paws like a rodeo
bull at the bowl of Fritos,
sharp pencil poised
to spear a slippery clue.

As a child I'd search
behind a huge TV
for the President's body
beaming into our house,
ruler of the Free World,
a king whose feet
did not touch ground.

Now I'm dueling with the man
who ordered armies to battle
and interns to bend over,
momentarily stuck
on a nine-letter
word for "infidelity."

That's when I flash
the finished puzzle
and a gloating grin
in his reddened face
and the ex-President,
barely lifting one cheek,
farts back.

Pandemic

No one noticing at first
subtle symptoms
on suburban streets,
random gestures
of total strangers,
here and there
a door held open,
directions given,
an involuntary smile.

But later, knowing
the viral path of
penguin to human,
rare and improbable,
panicked personnel
were powerless to prevent
a spreading contagion.
Too little, too late –

no drug
would stem this
outbreak's stride,
a frenzied breath
of love and forgiving
pouring down packed
highways, leaving behind
the infected ones, delirious,
overcome by their possessions,
abandoning cars and portfolios
in a fanatical hunger to comfort
the fortune-less,
houses turned out

like trouser pockets,
contents heaped in
curbside mounds,
money meaningless,
chaotic crowds
by the thousands
spilling forth their
hearts and purses
by the millions,

a scourge spanning oceans,
a global tide through
every tribe and village,
faith and color, families,
factions, clans, countries,
an all-consuming, incurable

kindness, soldiers
embracing, parliaments
emptied, borders
untended.
A clean sweep,
the tattered,
faded flag
of human nature,
life's tight, tense fabric
wholly unraveled,
formless and eased,
free to breathe
and weave,
anew.

Huevos Revueltos

Coarse bands of hard granite
once flat as sea-bottom
now fold and arch
like elephant skin
on a bare-rock mountain
named for the back
of a foreign beast
draped and curled
in graceful curves
proof enough
of nature's enduring
patience in softening
even the hardest places

even this gritty town
near my birth where
Old World neighbors
greet dark-skinned
newcomers with
grinding suspicion

and where the subtle
shift and bending of
bedrock might easily
be missed
one Sunday morning
in the local diner
as a friendly waitress
seats shy Salvadorans
trying their first meal
out in America

How d'ya say
"scrambled"

in Spanish?

I'm learning

she
smiles

huevos revueltos
huevos revueltos

Camel's Hump, Vermont /
Peekskill, New York

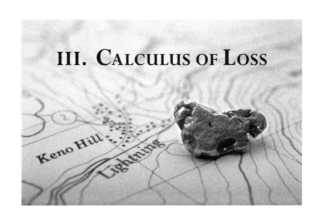

III. CALCULUS OF LOSS

Flood

If only I could drive an excavator
I need heavy equipment to dredge
through the silt and gravel of language
It will take a dozen bulldozers
to push enough words through my mouth
and return them to a shady rill
of sentences that I used to recognize
But so many adjectives
have been lost   swept away
and the only noun remaining
is water water water
My neighbor tries to speak
choking on water
The only verb is water
a chorus of water
wild screams of water
Speech lies soaking wet
useless and unsalvageable
The only dry ground
is silence where we stand
while giving the 'dozers time
to screech out a few words
buried under tons of stone
Until then we'll need
an earlier language
Let our fingers intertwine
and tired eyes meet and linger
Water might just return
to its proper place
if we wait long enough

until we can soothe
each other again
in a stunning waterfall
of fresh-rained tears

Breakfast with Buzz

for Buzz W.

Our scrambled conversation
runs like the sifting of bargain bins
at a rummage sale for cheap
stories, ones we hope might endure
beyond breakfast, beyond
the fringe of his fading memory.

I'm busy scanning my own headlines
for some startling news worth impressing
friends at this table, something to outlast
the forgettable food but today I'm just
finding comics, no sensational rescues
or brilliant op-eds, only bland humor
dished out with weak porridge
minus the real battles buried
on my back page, which is all
Buzz still reads these days,
his bold-faced, name-tag
banner headliner:
I am. I still am.

After the Flood

It's soon forgotten exactly where
in the scrambled landscape
the graceful willow
or rambling farmhouse
stood, the same way
Buzz puzzles
at the washed-out bridge
in his memory
that now separates him
from our conversation
seconds ago.
There's no return
once the storm
rips its path
through the familiar.
If only the past
could be dredged
like the tons of gravel
they shoved
from the bottom
of Route 4, hauled six
miles back up the mountain
from where it had poured
down just days before,
then paved to patch
the canyon-sized
gash in a highway artery.
But the heart has
no such heavy machinery.

What's lost can only
be worked by hand
a spadeful at a time,
in the one private garden
we each carefully tend.

Famine Grounds

Gentle hills, densely sown
with sugar beets to fatten
herds of hungry cattle –

soft-skinned land
enfolding a bone-hard past:
forty thousand bodies
tossed like cheap manure
on the fields by day,
by night a feast
for fox and badger.

Carts once carried
stacks of corpses
where a motorway
brings SUVs
from Cork and Cobh
and Carrigaline:
ancestral children's
children's children
commuting past
the Famine Grounds
toward pharmaceutical factories,
purging the world of maladies.

County Cork, Ireland

Rose

for Rose Loving,
in memory of Tom Stone

If only
we knew how
this tangled knot
unravels.

Next door
a huge mirror breaks
the same day
all your prayers
lie shattered
by a desert bullet.

There must have been
something to do
years ago to stop
this wheel today
from turning.

Oh, Rose,
could anyone
have named you better?

Can we ever
stretch a canvas
wide enough
to paint
your grief?

Brush us any color
you want,
let us

bleed
for you.

Teddi's Garden

for Teddi P.

The MRI reveals how
your body now tends
a wild and strange garden,
thriving tendrils
taking root in brain cells
that sowed a lifetime
of devotion
to all living things.

Such fertile soil, as if
cancer flowers,
and could it be
otherwise?

Love like this,
has no boundaries

Calculus of Loss

I heard of an old
hermit in Alaska
living near McCarthy,
scraped by six winters
in a makeshift tent
'til his wife finally
left him, still eats
alone each night
one can spaghetti
and one can beans
mixed and mashed
on a sheet-metal stove
into a perfect square,
cuts a bite
from one corner,
reshapes the rest
into another square,
takes a second bite
from another corner
and so on until
one more

evening is consumed
in the calculus of loss
which is how I imagine
consuming the past
if ever I should
have to lose you,

the constant stir
and thorough re-hash
like an unanswered prayer
chewed on word-by-word
until nothing remains
but the question itself,
the sharp-pointed bone of it,
impossible to swallow.

Moonlight

for Lynne H.

Because
a thing is named
moonlight   dying
I could believe
the thing is known

But one small pond
on one warm night
has spawned
a language
all its own
for *water*
loon   stillness
shimmering
and my *body*
softened
loose as sand
sifted gently
on a granite ledge
awash in satin
pools of light
amid the wild ones
shouting praises
to a stenographer moon
who madly scribes
their brilliant prose
into lines of stars
upon a page
of tonight's

unfinished story
her story

dying
in fading
constellations
inked behind
an approaching dawn

Nothing is Lost

Some morning
my missing keys
may clatter from
the tattered purse
of a startled Greek
widow arched over
a breadshop
counter

Or my fading tales
of romance might
be bundled and
sold to shy
Shanghai teens
on their first dates

Even these piano
riffs tossed out
like confetti could
rain down on
a puzzled farmer
in Bali pressing
clumps of sixteenth
notes deep into
warm loamy
rice paddy mud

And the thousand
names and places
slipped through

the mind's
worn pockets
every day
lie waiting
to be found again
sleek coins scattered
on the dusty playground
of tomorrow's memory

IV. ALMOST FORGIVEN

Oh Canada

Before gaining ground
in the geography of girls
I had a crush on Canada
as hopeless as my
fourth-grade crush
on Laura Jean
gently humming
her lyrical name
alone in my room
Oh Ca-na-da
while collecting stamps
and coveting them
like love notes posted
from wild bodies
of boreal forest
and barren tundra
laced with bays
of ice-rimmed indigo

I bore this love
through a simpler era
when we were raised
to love America
and only America
pledging the flag
with pious faith

But each school day
I would swear allegiance
like a secret traitor
never aware

of a fellow classmate
who knew he was gay
and could not reveal

how his body inhabited
a forbidden country
certain that no one
would ever care
to keep him among
their most cherished
collections

Above the Dental Office

From school each day
I'd return to a room
above the office
of my dentist father
over the piercing whine
of molars filled
and whimpering pleas
of children trapped
like cornered animals
and my father's voice
so caring and calm
and soothing as mint
drifting up through
ceiling cracks
with strains of muzak
in a muted soundtrack
for coming of age
during warm afternoons
of salacious groping
with a chain-smoking
girlfriend who soon
would leave me alone
in despair scorned for spitting
each time I French-kissed
her full luscious mouth
disgust and desire
and the shriek of the drill
all throbbing together
in the air of a room

where I first learned
it's possible to live with pain
or at least lie down
just a few feet above it

Winter Affair

Atop a ridge
of stunted spruce
and snow slabbed
five feet deep,
skimming solo across
a white birch draw
to a hidden glade
of fine February powder,
my secret lover,
snaking a slow descent
in a sinuous dance
down her smooth-sifted
forest floor, lured back
in the ravenous silence
and stiff caress
of a sharp west wind,
home-bound by
late-shadowed twilight
with red-faced
unfaithfulness,
amazed to see you
waiting still,
warm and lovely,
almost forgiven.

Amanita

Amanita's freckled face
beams with September dew
in crisp brown field grass
during a chilly walk
nearly crushing her
raucous yellow umbrella
The smallest bite

brings death or ecstasy,
warns a friend
Words from you

sometimes burst underfoot
like this bright fungus
with a bitter taste
rolled on the tongue
and swallowed hard,
full of dread
or promise
Last June

this same ground
blushed with the feast
of wild sweet
strawberries

Shopping Days

Swirling through a sea
of gloves and parkas
at LL Bean a few days
before Christmas
but my heart's not in it,
not since storming away
this morning drenched
in your accusations.

There's blood in the water,
in these aisles flooded
with shoppers lunging
at the scent of sales,
young staff staring
from their mountains
of student loans.

*Thirty years is more
than enough*, you cried,
whatever "enough" is.
I've never had enough
gloves or firewood or
enough sense of what
you need from me,
but after this bad
meal of a day
it's you I'm hungry for.

Let's clean our closets,
sell everything, start fresh.
I'll pay full price for you,
no more discounts.

Therapy

Alone and silent
with no common language
we arrive from separate planets
stranded on a short flight
from long-term commitment
Stepping inside we buckle down
with no sure destination
or hope for early departure
our seasoned pilot lifting off
toward wild dangerous worlds
of helpless humanoids
with peculiar traits
who we'll study
from a safe distance
as they struggle
with aberrant social
behavior remarkably
like our own

Jesus of Comcast

When our phone first went dead
I reached out in despair
to Customer Service on Live Chat:
Hello, came the instant message,
this is Jesus, how can I help you?
Now, I know what you're thinking
but please do not go there
although it crossed my mind too,
the shortest straw of a doubt
that indeed, I might
have once been blind
but now could see
gentle hands hovering
over our hundred-year-old
house and its slender thread
to the world-wide web.
Yet, whether from Oaxaca
or Nazareth, a miracle
truly did settle upon us that evening
in a subtle shift of electrons –
the phone resurrected,
our sins relieved.
And outside
in the cold crisp fall night,
bushels of bright stars
hung like ripe harvest fruit
while back inside,
faith restored,
you and a vintage red wine
stood beckoning again,
full-bodied and brilliant.

Love

This little loaf of a word
is never enough to pass around
and any way you cut it
I can see through
even the thickest slice.

Give me a grand metaphor
for something that
can't be missed,
whether achingly large,
like a flood-ravaged city
left hungry and abandoned.

Or small and furtive,
like a dark-eyed creature
caught in the glare
of snow-slanted headlights.

Or maybe something in between –
where we find ourselves
sitting now, for instance –
at a silent dinner table
with spoons in hand,
weighing the contents
of each look and gesture
like unopened letters
from a familiar address.

Budget

An anatomy of numbers
awaits dissection
splayed out on paper
like a limp frog
in biology lab

It takes queasy courage
to cleave lines between
eating-in and eating-out
slice open veins of income
isolate fatty deposits
of extra cash

No doubt a test will follow
a final reckoning
by the kitchen table
of what we gave
and what was given
over several decades
parsing wallet and purse
for the living muscle
of our genuine wealth
in uncounted blessings

So let's lean hard into our work
like researchers on the verge
of a great discovery
or as Mayan priests
prepared to lift a beating heart
from the sacred body
of our life together

an offering to any god
or financial planner
whichever we may
meet with first

Virgin Mary

Her favorite figurine
now a sad pile of broken
blue-and-white porcelain
heaped on the counter
and my wife implores a
resurrection be performed
by me
a simple Jew
armed only with Super Glue
and trepidation
but setting mind and jaw
squarely to the task
of all mankind
I do manage restoring
her slightly-cracked
sly smile
to its proper place
the same smile
that smashed me open
more than thirty years ago
still thrilling in random glances
over a sandwich or pillow
and though we've been broken
a few times as may happen
to most things brittle
when hit by something hard
the scattered china
always beckons us
to the bare floor
on bent knees

searching eye-to-eye
under chair and table
for the missing piece
with jagged hands
sparkling blue-and-white
and soft in prayer

V. TASTING PRECIOUS METAL

Gathering

In the beginning
was glacial rock
gathered into stony soil
which gathered these maples
which now gather us
gathering fresh sap
as March air softens
slabs of deep snow,
stumbling on snowshoes
toward the steamy arch
with buckets brimming
buzzing like honeybees
around a sweet boiling brew,
waking from winter's isolation
with home-made wine
and ginger snaps,
fleece jackets unzipped
by a blazing firebox
gathering the hours,
gathering news and tales
of friends in need,
gathering time
in boiled-down years
toward a moment
of distillation
that gathers the best
we can bring to each other,
liquid treasure poured
thick and sweet,
a glowing amber
cherished in the brilliant
April morning light.

Cake

Six-thirty near sunset on a
summer Sunday evening
seventy-seven degrees and
clear cruising east on 107 to
George's birthday party he is
seventy-one and this central
Vermont valley is lit like his
birthday cake all seventy-plus
candles glowing and sparking
hayfields and maples and
town hall clock tower and
Cumberland Farms and
John Dutton on his bicycle
looking more than ever
like Ichabod Crane yes
the whole movie on fire
my radio registering
the mood with a blazing
soundtrack while
the landscape burns
its brilliant way
through the day's
end   And

just this morning
about four thousand feet
higher than here after huddling
on a craggy clump
atop Mount Moosilauke
with a sleety sideways rain
soaking soggy lunches and
any meager chance of viewing

sunlit valleys below
our mad bunch of
mud-caked muskrats
slogged a giggly retreat
down flash-flooded trails
to chips and cold beer   But

back here bathed
in the warmth of
George's flaming cake
crowning hills now
and blowing west across
the planet blessedly
beyond control I'll

soon rejoin these same
drenched companions
newly washed and
wine-soaked and we will
share a slice or two of cake
as the flames of our days
flicker and flare and
I will know it today
beyond all doubt and
time that yes

This is Beauty
This is Love

Grazing

Stalking wild strawberries
satisfies the animal in me
knee-sore face-down bare-assed hunting
for plump small drops of summer juice

I'd do it all day if they'd hire me
clocking in at dawn with a few lazy deer
in tall meadow grass swapping bad jokes
and beer for hours until sent our separate ways
by dew-darkened dusk

the deer dancing off under warm stars
while I stagger home drunk and happy
dreaming of elusive past lovers
gathered in sweet moist handfuls
of wild illicit snacks

A Bat Is Living

The faint soft rustle
flutters like dragonflies
in a dark cramped cavity
of the bow
A bat

is living in my canoe

Probably nested there under the shed roof
since March then three rough hours
on a car rack to this first paddle
of spring

Only the two of us out here
on stillwater rousing from winter
drumming wingbeats against
a mist-and-cedar-rimmed shore
flaming in sunrise

Snake Skin

A snake skin
is only a snake skin
until given
to the ten-year-old
who has barely begun
to trust in you

He too
may shed some doubts
like translucent scales
from his troubled heart

and peel you too
with his searching look
back to something
forgotten but true
in nature's fragile design
held weightless and shimmering
in his restless young eyes

Some day you pray
you both may climb
with grace and ease
from these clumsy skins
in tall lush grass
and slip away

Laptop

I gaze at the glossy
device, stroke its smooth
gleaming skin –
a sleek silver fish
asleep on the desk.

Awakened,
this wild creature
pulses under my fingers,
a playful dolphin darting
and diving in the immense
ocean of connectivity
where we swim together
through nets and portals
or within silent dark cafes,
floating among schools
of flickering faces
searching vast pools
of our common knowledge
in hope of still finding
spawning grounds
left untouched

Handball

My friend Allyn once fought
some wicked handball
with a worthy rival
so closely matched
an hour's play found them
tied twelve even
when a lean hard serve
split the ball exactly
in half   offered now
like two halves
of sweet-ripened
fruit savored
as we reunite
at a banquet
celebrating all times
when something
somewhere
broke perfectly apart
just so we might
start anew
scores forgotten

Recipe for Relaxing with Men

A fire, first and foremost
in two sizes, big and bigger
Not for warmth or want,
hell no —
to poke, prod,
pile, and piss on,
something to do,
something to watch,
the doing and watching
fueled by flasks of whiskey
and the Sierra-lit summer night sky,
canopy of galaxies over a glacial lake
slate-smooth and moss-still.

All of this must simmer
in the chicken stock
of sadness,
thick and sweet,
savored and anonymous,
the silent soup within which
all men stir.

Let enough time pass
soaking slowly
in the quiet of the night,
a splendid isolation
oozing around each man.

Then and only then,
light as a soufflé,
talk rises and floats

and bursts in bubbles and burps,
small talk and stupid and dumb,
lewd and funny
of coincidence and conquest
advice   adventure
mistakes   self-censure
autos and animals
sports   spirits
and body parts,
an endless spiral
of randomness
as forgettable as bad TV.
Flavorful and warm,
this talk wraps around
and around and around
the grounded gathering of
full-bellied, empty-minded men
relaxing.

Old friends

Emerging from our tents
familiar as a load of laundry
drawn from the dryer,
fresh, well-worn,
a little rumpled,
we greet the Adirondack
August morning light.

Before this weekend
nearly thirty years
plodding a beaten path
between our open doors.

Before that
our own orbits
in other marriages.

Before that
our families,
the fickle climate
and loamy ground
of our first flowering,
bits and pieces
still scattered

about this campsite.
Look, what I've found,
casually shared over coffee —
the craggy, jagged
fragment of memory

turned gently to the light
in a cupped hand.

Breakfast dishes
left unwashed,
we lie cleansed
by languid
lake and loon song,
comforted, content,
prepared for
summer rain or
whatever may
come our way.

Little Tupper Lake, Adirondack region

Tractor Man

Fifteen summers I've passed you
on the same stretch of dirt road
back behind the Third Branch
of the White River, a bedraggled
lump of wild beard and splayed
knees stuffed onto your tiny
worn-out lawn tractor stuck in
first gear, sputter-crawling four miles
from town to a hardscrabble
farmhouse with empty barn and
hayfields long gone to seed.
I go there to run, to coax
another season's cycle from
an aging body slowed down
a notch each year, loping
by without a word, my hand
tossed out in a humble wave
hardly masking a smug sense
of agility and superior fitness.
So we pass,

and time passes both the hare
and the tortoise, slumped further
into your John Deere shell, beard
grown shaggier though in my heart
I know we shall cross the same finish
line, you and I, someday with our
perfect bodies and breathless faces
glowing pink with purpose
and pride, a job well done.

Dancing Girls

Seven men in a rented van
out for a night-on-the-town
in Montreal, flying north
through late November
stark-slanted shadows
past pale cornfields,
abandoned hay bales,
then piling out on a gravel

shoulder pit-stop
bursting with bad jokes,
chilled by sharp stinging
swipes of eighteen-wheelers,

until all eyes tilt toward
the rose-tinged sky's
tremorous chatter —

rivers of geese in
swollen floodways,
shimmering veins
of sinuous bodies
pulsing southward
overhead, over
these aging men
oddly aroused,

migration on hold,
heads raised
in murmured embrace
of the airborne
dancing
girls.

Playground

Consider the child
who awakens happy,
primed and charged
to seize the gift
of each new day.

Watch how the sun
excites her
and her friends
bouncing bruised
and battered
like free electrons,
un-deterred
by solid objects.

Imagine the origin
of our Universe,
the cosmic burst
of nascent energy
expanding out past
countless galaxies
to these pink-faced,
laughing, pig-tailed
specks of scattered
star dust swirling
through the maple-
slanted morning light.

Chickadees

In this deep cold
cave of January
the house beams settle
with a cracking thud
like an empty pint
slammed down
on a pub counter

I could use a refill about now

Daylight's running low
and the snow tires
have a better grip on things
than my slipping sanity

Thank god for the chickadees
those little truck-stop waitresses
shrugging off winter's
dismal tips while
going about their business
with eternal cheerfulness

A little more coffee or tea tea tea?

Honestly now

Campsite as cathedral:
corky, rooted columns,
a thousand vestibules to choose
for coffee and blessings.

Morning lightshafts
slice through air
so thick it fuses
with lake and land.
My breath takes in all as one
rich foamy, loamy ether.

Ospreys whistle,
pages turn.

To know all this, fully,
means to die.

What a relief
to wash a bowl,
change socks,
filter water.

Honestly now,
where do we go from here?

Lake Lila, Adirondack region

Hummingbird

A deep canyon of the Yuba
seared by Sierra's summer torch,
high-country snowmelt
hoarded in white granite pools.

Dipped and cooled,
mind and body
forged and naked,
with a tempered cleanse
and open heart, I hold

Hummingbird, or rather
Hummingbird holds me
under tiny claws,
a fragrant liquid
in a fragile,
feathered teacup.

If I hold you toe to finger,
wildly precious and
delicately adored, if

I hold you with a
weightless touch,
a cautious contact
riding my finger
leaf to leaf,
gentle passenger
with wings at rest,
tongue at work
lapping nectar, if

I hold you eye to eye
sizing one another,
mutually stunned, if

I hold you, already gone
in a subtle stir of
canyon breath and
whirring blink of
wingbeats, how

shall we color
this trust?

South Fork of the Yuba River,
Nevada County, California

Keno Hill, 1972

Three hundred miles
from nowhere driving drunk
late Saturday night
down a snow-crusted highway
from Keno Hill Bar
to the miners' bunkhouse
nearly ten below
and there's a single shoe
left in the empty road soon
followed by another shoe
socks shirt pants jacket all
shed like snake skin by a kid
staggering in the high-beams
high on speed blue-faced
and babbling like a newborn
so we bundle him back safe
that night to shiver through
another day in the mines
where he pretends not to
know us and though we all
say he's crazy truth is you
can understand the hunger
for lightness and a fresh crisp
start from here in the Far North
sprinting naked into your own
wild roadless future with nothing
heavier on your mind than the
complete and utterly dismal
absence of any woman

Yukon Territory

A destination first takes shape in the mouth,
syllables rolled together like gold nuggets
in a sluice box and gathered into a feast
of dust-choked highway until one
evening you find yourself alone
outside a mine shaft on night shift,
your hard-hat beam no match
for a burst of Northern Lights
and wolf howls. You are
in the spring of your life,
your name still a destination
for others yet to be born,
with only a lunchbox
at midnight
to tide you over
to another arctic dawn.
How is it
that two feet can track
through a billion
stars so the eyes
may follow later?
Look – now –
where you've been,
where you once thrashed
through thick brush
like a grazing animal.
It's all that remains,
this trampled grass,
a taste of precious metal.

NOTES

"Stone Wall," page 22. On the morning of September 24, 1995, three friends and I broke camp at the edge of the tiny village of Dhotarap. We had been trekking two weeks through the legendary land of Dolpo in the high Himalayas of northwestern Nepal, a rugged and spectacular region seldom visited by Westerners, made famous by Peter Matthieson's popular 1972 journal, *The Snow Leopard*. Urche (Ur-chay), a marvelous ten-year-old goat-herder whom we'd met just the day before, ran into camp to say good-bye. We had been delighted by Urche's brief visits and couldn't stop talking about his warm enthusiasm, boundless energy and clever antics. We also knew there was almost no opportunity to receive a good education in this remote corner of Nepal. But a random act of kindness was about to change all that. In a wild impulse I proposed to my friends that we co-sponsor Urche at a boarding school in the city of Kathmandu, worlds apart from his mountain home in Dolpo. Amazingly, they all agreed. And so began an extraordinary relationship of nearly twenty years that has expanded to affect the lives of dozens – perhaps hundreds – of people in a dozen nations around the world.

"Dipika's Walk," page 27. During a visit to Nepal in April of 2006, the People's Democracy Movement had paralyzed the country with general strikes and huge street demonstrations, demanding an end to a brutal 10-year civil war and the reinstatement of parliament, which had been dissolved by an unpopular king. Tensions ran high as close to a million people poured into the streets to confront the army and the king, with the grim possibility of peaceful demonstrations turning into a bloodbath. But at the last minute, the king backed down and there were celebrations instead, the movement eventually toppling the royal family and giving the country its first historic step toward becoming a secular democracy. Dipika was a remarkable girl we met on the same trip, residing at a home for disabled children.

"Flood," page 38. On August 28-29, 2011, parts of central and southern Vermont were hit by Tropical Storm Irene, some valleys receiving more than seven inches of rain in less than 24 hours, causing catastrophic damage and altering the landscape.

"Rose," page 44. Sergeant Tom Stone, 52, died March 29, 2006 in Afghanistan in a friendly fire incident, leaving behind his fiancé, Rose Loving, of

Tunbridge, Vermont. He was serving his third volunteer tour of duty as a medic with the Vermont National Guard. Tom's personal mission was to provide health services in remote rural villages using a mobile clinic he had fashioned out of an 8'x12' shipping container. To honor his memory, donations have gone toward building several schools in isolated villages of Afghanistan. For more information go to: http://www.directaidinternational.org/.

ABOUT THE AUTHOR

Danny Dover lives with his wife, Mary Swartz, in a remodeled school-house in Bethel, Vermont. He received his B.A. from Antioch College in 1971 and also holds Associate Degrees in Surveying Technology and Keyboard Technology. Danny was the piano technician at Dartmouth College for seventeen years and continues servicing pianos part-time. Previously he worked as a folk singer, contradance musician, dulcimer-maker, foundry patternmaker, and surveyor. Danny serves on the Board of *Hands in Outreach, Inc.,* a small non-profit group coordinating educational sponsorships for very poor children in Nepal (http://www.handsinoutreach.org/). His poems have appeared in *Blueline* and numerous issues of *Bloodroot Literary Magazine*. He has published one chapbook, *Kindness Soup, Thankful Tea* (Dhotarap Press, 2006). Danny was a 2013 Pushcart nominee.

This book has been set in Perpetua, designer Eric Gill's most celebrated typeface. The clean, chiseled look of this font reflects its creator's stone-cutting work.

To order additional copies of this book or other Antrim House titles, contact the publisher at

Antrim House
21 Goodrich Rd., Simsbury, CT 06070
860.217.0023, AntrimHouse@comcast.net
or the house website (www.AntrimHouseBooks.com).

•

On the house website
in addition to information on books
you will find sample poems, upcoming events,
and a "seminar room" featuring supplemental biography,
notes, images, poems, reviews, and
writing suggestions.